A QUESTION OF RACE

The report of a conference on
the future of mental health services
for the black communities held at
the City University, London on
19 and 20 September 1990.

Compiled by Carol Baxter

Edited by Yvonne Christie and Linda Moore

Community Living Development Team
King's Fund Centre

Published by the King's Fund Centre
126 Albert Street
London
NW1 7NF
Tel: 071 267 6111

ISBN   1 85717 000 8

Distributed by Bailey Distribution Ltd
Dept KFP
Learoyd Road
Mountfield Industrial Estate
New Romney
Kent
TN28 8XU

The King's Fund Centre is a health services development agency which promotes improvements in health and social care. We do this by working with people in health services, in social services, in voluntary agencies, and with the users of their services. We encourage people to try out new ideas, provide financial or practical support to new developments, and enable experiences to be shared through workshops, conferences and publications. Our aim is to ensure that good developments in health and social care are widely taken up.

 The King's Fund Centre is part of the King Edward's Hospital Fund for London

CONTENTS

Appendices

ACKNOWLEDGEMENTS

My sincere thanks and love go to the working party for the conference – namely, Adrian, Arunjot, Juliana, Loraine, Mike and Peter. Without their help, thought and input, we would never have got things together in time. Thanks also for their assistance on the days of the conference.

Appreciation goes to the facilitators and special thanks to Loraine for stepping into Stephanie Gabriel's shoes. She filled them brilliantly under extreme short notice!

Grateful thanks to Carol Baxter for her compilation of the whole event – she did the conference justice.

Thanks also to Linda Moore for assisting me in re-editing, re-typing and preparing the report for publication. To Melanie Kornitzer for co-ordinating all the application forms, cheques and cash, and, last but not least, thank you to all who attended and participated in the two days and for their patience in awaiting this report.

Yvonne Christie
The King's Fund Centre
22 April 1991

FOREWORD

In common with the rest of the National Health Service, mental health services are facing difficult times. For black users of the services, these difficulties are nothing new. Not only are they subjected to the stigmas attached to mental illness, but they are the victims of racism. The uneven use of mental illness services, the over-representation of black people in certain caseloads (schizophrenia being the most common) and the differential rates of use of therapies such as Electro Convulsive Therapy (ECT), are just a few examples of the failure of existing services to make an appropriate response to the needs of black people. More worryingly the way in which professional dominance has perpetuated this lack of response to date is an indication of the type of problem that needs to be tackled.

The strongest feeling gained by observers of the service is that of failure. Little or no effort has been made to involve black users in determining the shape and content of the services they receive. This is the case even among the majority of 'innovative' projects promoting the user view and self advocacy. Is it any wonder, then, that there is a deep distrust of psychiatric medicine in all its many manifestations? Black people have not been allowed the opportunity to participate on an equal basis, either as individuals or through the many locally based community groups which exist to advocate their views.

It is ironic then that in a number of places both the statutory sector and many of the large national voluntary organisations have placed an added burden upon black community groups. Not only do these groups have to act as campaigners for equality, they must also meet the shortcomings of others. All this within ever decreasing budgets, and a consequence of the National Health Service and Community Care Bill, a totally new basis for funding. The need for fundamental change is patently evident. What those changes should be and how to bring them about is a concern of the Community Living Development Team of the King's Fund Centre. A number of initiatives are being planned in an attempt to shift both perception and practice.

The King's Fund is well known as an information resource. The Community Living Development Team is developing this resource, bringing into the networks black groups and individuals, who can provide both information and be used as sounding boards for ideas, thus developing concepts such as participation and collaboration. The team is also establishing and maintaining links with innovative projects in the statutory sector and among national and local voluntary organisations.

A number of development projects have been set up, focusing on the issues arising from the NHS and Community Care Bill. the consequent changes. As well as encouraging change the King's Fund plays an important role in evaluating new schemes and disseminating new ideas.

I was involved last year in organising a one day event which focused on the implications of contracts for the mental health services for the black communities. It was clear from this conference that there was a need for a further conference in order to bring together a wider network of black people nationally, to look at what shape and form services would be required in the future.

It is essential that, as black people, we are prepared for the changes ahead, and that we are prepared for the opportunities and challenges which these changes will bring.

We hope this report will provide a springboard for action for better mental health services for the black (and indeed for all) communities.

Yvonne Christie
Senior Project Officer
King's Fund Centre

TERMINOLOGY

Throughout this document the term 'black' is used because the term 'ethnic minorities' is not acceptable to the wider black communities, and a number of people so labelled have told us that they find the term offensive.

INTRODUCTION

BACKGROUND TO THE CONFERENCE

The contents of this report are based on a conference, The Future of Mental Health Services for The Black Communities which was held on 19 and 20 September 1990 at the City University, London. The conference was organised by Yvonne Christie, Senior Project Officer at the King's Fund Centre. It was aimed specifically at service users as well as service providers in both the statutory and voluntary sectors.

The conference was planned as an event for, and facilitated by, black people. This was to enable participants to feel at ease and to express their feelings openly without being constrained by the presence of white people. For this purpose the event was widely advertised through a variety of community organisations and media and an ethnicity monitoring questionnaire used with an application form.

It was well-attended and a list of participants is contained in Appendix D.

FORMAT OF THE CONFERENCE

On the morning of day one, two speakers set the scene by focusing on different aspects of the issues around mental health and the black communities. There was then a short period for questions and input from the participants.

The late morning and afternoon session were devoted to workshops addressing the issues of:

✦ Black women and mental health

✦ Alternative therapies

✦ Perspectives of the NHS and Community Care Act

- ✦ Mental health and the elderly
- ✦ Supporting and involving families in the community.

The second day addressed the issues of the voluntary and statutory services working together.

THE AIM OF THIS REPORT

In addition to reporting on the proceedings of the conference, this report is intended to provide a firm starting point from which readers can take up and develop the issues raised. A comprehensive reading list is included to assist readers to develop their knowledge and awareness (Appendix E).

YVONNE CHRISTIE, PROJECT OFFICER, COMMUNITY LIVING DEVELOPMENT TEAM, KING'S FUND CENTRE

CONFERENCE ORGANISER'S INTRODUCTION

In her opening remarks to the conference, Yvonne Christie said that with a background in the voluntary sector she had developed strengths and skills in working with the community. The best way in which she can justify her position in the King's Fund Centre is by keeping her feet in both camps. In this way, she will be better able to inform the King's Fund Centre of those things which it can do to push forward the issues of race and mental health.

She reminded participants that service planners often ignore black people. It was for this reason that the aims of the conference were:

✦ to bring together black people who are working in, or concerned about, the field of mental health to focus their attention on their role in shaping future services;

✦ for participants to share their experience, knowledge and skills to re-affirm their strength as a people;

✦ to highlight the King's Fund Centre's commitment to the role of mental health services for the black communities.

She called for participants to draw on the wealth of creativity and sensitivity of black people when putting forward their contributions.

MESSAGE FROM THE ORGANISER

I believe there are many injustices put upon men and women from the black communities.

I believe that workers in the field of mental health have a lot to learn from members of the black communities.

I believe that our voices must be as one, to be at their most powerful for effective change.

I believe we can bring about the kind of transformation which will be beneficial to us all.

This conference can be the start ...

We must attend with open hearts and minds to explore and acknowledge our achievements.

We need to recognise that as a people we have power, we are creative and we are unique. As our histories have shown us:

TOGETHER WE STAND
BUT UNITED WE WILL NEVER FALL!

ONE LOVE

JOSEPHINE KWAHLI, DIRECTOR OF SOCIAL DIVISION, FOCUS CONSULTANCY

OVERVIEW OF SERVICES IN BRITAIN FOR THE BLACK COMMUNITIES

Josephine Kwahli welcomed the opportunity of a conference for black people involved in mental health services to discuss issues that affected people both as workers and clients. She emphasised that racism and the struggle against it were the starting point.

She described the economic and ideological roots of racism: the greed for trade, money, land and labour led to the subjugation of black people by white people. The myth of white superiority and black inferiority was developed as an ideology to justify this. This same ideology is used today against black people, when we are told we should be happy to accept poor services.

Black people receive inferior service and care in the field of mental health as well as in other aspects of society. We know that mental health services don't cater well for many other people – white working class people also get a bad deal – but the effects of racism worsens the position for black people. How many more studies are needed before white service providers will accept that this is an issue?

THE DILEMMA OF BLACK SERVICE PROVIDERS

Since its inception in 1948, the NHS has exploited black people as cheap labour. The demand by black people for appropriate services and care has given a new twist to this situation. In response to our assertion for appropriate services, service providers employ black people to deal with the problem rather than examining their policies and procedures. This gives black service providers a dilemma: we are given two jobs: to describe the problem; and, in isolation, to solve the problem. Is the role of white service providers to serve white Europeans only – or should they also serve black people?

WHAT IS CHANGE?

Black service providers undoubtedly have a key role as agents of change. The question, however, is whether white people want to hand over influence and power, and whether they are prepared to accept the integrity of black people and to work towards change. Race Units, Equal Opportunities Policies, an increase in the employment of black specialist staff, and the awareness of white liberals are quoted as evidence. But the imprisoning and incarceration of our community has not changed, nor has the low salary and low status of black people within organisations. Individual achievements are relatively unimportant. What is important is continued collective action as part of a broader black social movement.

In conclusion, Ms Kwahli asked what is really meant by mental health, especially when our very response to racism and prejudice is interpreted as insanity and when the existing institutions are set up to validate that oppression. What is surprising, she said, is not that there are so many who suffer, but that there are so many of us who don't.

Mental health is part of that broader struggle. So much time is spent trying to convince people of racism that we neglect the time we need to think creatively. We need our energy and time to think about what the new structure of services could look like.

DR AGGREY BURKE, CONSULTANT PSYCHIATRIST, ST GEORGE'S HOSPITAL, LONDON

PSYCHIATRIC PRACTICE AND MENTAL HEALTH

In his opening remarks, Dr Burke acknowledged the common experience of the Caribbean and Asian communities as the two major racial and cultural minority communities in Britain.

THE CONCEPT OF DEPRIVATION

A demographic perspective focusing on areas such as employment, housing and education shows that black people experience greater levels of deprivation than the use of services would indicate. We need to be concerned about the destructive effect of deprivation on our communities. It is a process which leaves us with a sense of neglect and a feeling that we are somehow to blame for our lack of decent housing, unemployment or low paid jobs, and inadequate education services. This deprivation can affect us in different ways. It causes many of us to feel confused and to become withdrawn and it causes others to become involved in riots and other disturbances. These are two responses to the effects of deprivation.

Dr Burke referred to two studies he is currently involved with in his post as Consultant Psychiatrist. The first is on mothers and children in care. About 60 per cent of children in care in London are African-Caribbean. These children are less likely to be placed with families and are therefore more likely than white children in care to be in children's homes and other institutions. The majority of mothers and children in the study were African-Caribbean. High levels of stress, lack of support and poor living conditions were experienced by the families involved.

The second study covers twenty youngsters and here there was evidence of considerable psychological disturbance. Factors such as insecurity within the family, time in care, abuse, hospitalisation and the experience of the juvenile justice system were prevalent. The study showed that the girls were as psychologically disturbed as the boys. One third of the sample were very disturbed. The results of this study suggest the need for supportive intervention at an earlier stage – rather than when people become psychologically disturbed.

The experiences of people who contact a telephone advice service were cited by Dr Burke as further evidence of a need for early support. The desperation and despair of people who are constantly thwarted in their efforts to find work, and the physical harassment and abuse faced by black people on the street were common experiences of callers.

Dr Burke then described the path to mental health services as having five levels. Level one is the family. People move from there to the GP, to the Social Services department, to being a voluntary inpatient, then to the fifth level of being locked up. There is a significant over-representation of black people at the fifth level. Black people are locked away in care, in secure units and in prisons. It is understandable that most of the concern of the black communities has focused at this level. However, there is a lot of work to be done at the earlier levels. If our expertise, creativity and perspective were directed at earlier levels of intervention, we could achieve more positive results and benefit a larger number of black people.

While society is divided along racial grounds, there will be no change and the lock up reality for black people will remain. Finally, Dr Burke reinforced Josephine Kwahli's earlier point by arguing that at present there is an offloading of black issues onto black service providers.

QUESTIONS AND INPUT FROM PARTICIPANTS
Discussion centred mainly around alternative approaches. Some of the points raised included:

✦ the issue of black people's acceptance of white psychiatrists;

✦ the dilemma of working in racist organisations.

These points were felt to be important and should be continuously addressed.

Participants felt that attention in our communities is often focused on opposition to the locking up of black people in prisons and mental institutions. One reason for this is the fact that the alternatives for the earlier levels of prevention are difficult, draining and protracted. The need to look at mental health, not mental illness and to place more emphasis on prevention was reiterated. A practising acupuncturist made reference to the role of acupuncture in promoting mental health and identified its scope and limitations.

The development of the Hackney Afro-Caribbean Mental Health Programme is in its final planning stages. This programme will be carried out by black volunteers and statutory workers. The emphasis will be on alternative approaches, including therapies. People's experience of racism will be actively addressed.

In referring to notions and interpretation around change, participants were urged to recognise their abundant strength and creativity as a people. If we apply this, we can come up with useful responses to effect change.

WORKSHOP REPORTS

At the start of each workshop, participants were given a grounding on key issues of concern. Following the workshop, there was feedback from each group, highlighting the salient points of their discussion. Presentations were delivered in a variety of innovative ways. The highlights being short 'skits' based on African/Caribbean mythology (Anansi and the Elephant and a tragedy/comedy drama of a family's encounter with Section 136 and the police). It is not possible to give any real flavour of these presentations. However, these approaches avoided repetition and made good use of the limited time available. Moreover, they were powerful ways of making some simple but important statements. The principal themes and issues which emerged are as follows.

PERSPECTIVES ON THE NHS AND COMMUNITY CARE ACT 1990

Facilitators: Safder Mohammed and Loraine Martins

There has been very little consultation with black communities and what little there has been has proved tokenistic. Implications of the Act for the communities were identified under the following three headings.

Contracts

✦ Black organisations are at a disadvantage in the contractual process. Many are very small, under-resourced and deprived of the secure managerial and financial base required to enter into contracts with statutory organisations.

✦ Advocacy and campaigning roles are not recognised in service contracts. This poses a threat to the funding of campaigning services.

✦ Housing Associations need to link into the discussions around contracts.

Assessment

✦ Assessment is based on a medical model and is made by white professionals. Socio-political factors such as poverty, racism and cultural differences are not taken into account.

✦ The "professionalisation" of black service providers may mean they cannot offer support to black users. "How well do you know your people and yourselves?" is a question which was constantly raised.

Care plans

✦ There is no guarantee that care plans will reflect local need.

✦ A greater emphasis should be placed on alternative approaches and on prevention in care plans.

SUPPORTING AND INVOLVING FAMILIES IN THE COMMUNITY

Facilitators: Mike Zamora and Lydia Yee

✦ The contribution of carers is not recognised, especially in the planning of services.

✦ Carers do not have access to information about important issues such as the benefits and side-effects of medication. More information is also needed about carers' rights. Medical terminology is confusing and there is inadequate information about access to services.

✦ Carers have no choice in the services offered and are simply expected 'to take it or leave it'.

✦ Professional attitudes towards carers were not supportive, especially from older General Practitioners with little experience of working in the mental health field.

- ✦ The type and quality of rehabilitation facilities are inadequate, causing a subsequent burden on the family.

- ✦ Statutory services only work between the hours of 9 and 5. There is the need for support outside these hours.

- ✦ Sections 2 and 136 of the Mental Health Act are easily manipulated by the police who often request unsuspecting relatives to take the client outside their residence where it is then possible to apply Section 136 – removal to a 'place of safety'. The interpretation of 'safety' is a hospital or cell.

- ✦ There was some debate about whether black voluntary organisations should be seen as a place of safety. The main concern is that they could become a dumping ground for black clients.

- ✦ Carers are caught in the institutional friction between health authorities and social services departments. The black voluntary sector which supported carers is shrinking, leaving them with no support.

ALTERNATIVE THERAPIES

Facilitator: Mark I

- ✦ This workshop felt that there was little information available on this area.

- ✦ Reference was made to the use of acupuncture and acupressure. The value of such forms of alternative therapy in mental health is often not believed or understood.

- ✦ The tradition of healing in our communities, for example spiritual treatment, must be recognised.

The term 'alternative' itself needs much thought and discussion. People present felt that the term 'alternative' gives the impression that black people are prescribing some fringe, unorthodox method(s) of treatment. In fact, therapies to be used, widely explored and monitored include some of the very therapies that are available to certain factions of the wider, often middle-class, white community.

Successful alternative therapies include:

+ acupuncture
+ acupressure
+ psychodrama
+ art therapy
+ psychotherapy
+ counselling
+ group therapy.

Unfortunately, 'folk-lore' has rendered the use of such practices as 'unsuitable for the black community'. This myth must not only be challenged and these methods of practice become widely available as a serious alternative, but there must also be a series of case studies involving monitoring and evaluation in order to test their success over a decent period of time alongside the 'mainstream' medical models of practice.

BLACK WOMEN AND MENTAL HEALTH

Facilitator: Arunjot Mushiana

> *Every woman's mental health is affected by the way her society regards and treats unmarried women, childless women, mothers, poor women, assaulted women, divorced women, minority women, disabled women, widows, aged women or women with aspirations.*
> Pathiel (1987): Women and Mental Health. A post-Nairobi Perspective. World Health Statisics. Quart. 40.

The workshop looked at a few case studies describing black women's experience and expression of mental distress. Society exacerbates suffering due to mental distress by the very nature of its racist structure, leaving women in a state of total helplessness. Many women develop coping strategies which are impressive under the circumstances, but these too often prove to be maladaptive in the long-term. Effective therapy, therefore, would be invaluable to enable the development of appropriate skills. However, most therapists hold world views so disparate with those of the black women, that it is often seen as 'inappropriate' or 'too difficult', so medical intervention is used instead which only further disables the person. In addition, clinicians may come to hold negative stereotypes, attributing stress-related emotional problems to class and culture, and totally disregarding the impact that racism has on our mental health, as well as the effect of the suffering we see inflicted on our families and communities which strips us of our dignity.

Positive mental well-being is the product of a stable supportive environment. The following model was put forward to describe the intensity of black women's lives which caused many to experience episodes of acute loneliness and depression due to the inadequacies in basic resources.

The diagram best describes issues raised at the workshop and is a reflection of women's feelings on this issue.

The way forward in alleviating such anxiety in black womens lives is through the development of appropriate and sensitive services, involving these women at every stage in planning and in their delivery. Advocacy schemes would further enable women to access complex bureaucracy.

MENTAL HEALTH AND THE ELDERLY

Facilitator: Dr Pearl Hetteriarchy

Over the next ten years, there will be an increase in black people of pensionable age in Britain. According to OPCS data there are 395,000 people who were born outside the UK and who are of pensionable age. By the end of the century this figure is expected to have increased to one million. Although some research has been carried out, little is known about the extent of mental ill health among our elders.

Elderly black people often have more difficulty in gaining access to services because of language barriers. Research also shows that, because of the constant struggle of their daily life, black people appear to suffer disability and ill health at an earlier age. This is often further compounded by their unrealised dream of returning home.

Black elders do not have access to services such as home helps and meals-on-wheels because they do not know about them or because these services are inappropriate.

Although many black doctors specialise in psychogeriatrics, they tend to work in areas of the country which are predominantly white.

Some examples of small but very creative schemes and initiatives developed by black organisations and individuals are as follows:

✦   a black elderly man has opened up his house to give baths to other local elderly people

✦   a Pakistani family in Camden provides 'meals-on-legs' to elderly people

- a group of black people in Greenwich demanded their own food in meals-on-wheels, and the service is now contracted in
- a Camden scheme for Chinese elders has a mixed age facility to aid other roles of elders (such as grandparents).

Dr Hettiarchy is one of the few people who has valid information on the needs of the black elderly. She is particularly keen to ensure that services do address the particular needs of the elderly. In the health field, people often omit to campaign for this group, due largely to the lack of information on black senior citizens' changing needs.

Participants felt that this workshop was very informative and had highlighted issues they were keen to learn more about.

VOLUNTARY AND STATUTORY SERVICES WORKING TOGETHER

Opening remarks by Loraine Martins (standing in for Stephanie Gabriel)

Over the last decade we have seen a shift in the roles of local authorities, health authorities and the voluntary sector. The language of services has changed: 'market place', 'purchasing', 'contracts', 'value for money' are now the priorities for health and local authorities.

While more demands are being placed on voluntary services, they have less resources. Many voluntary organisations are not even aware of the resources which are available to them. Voluntary services also face the dilemma of providing services which the State should supply. They are seen as the poor relations and are constantly expected to justify their continued funding. Their contribution is rarely recognised and there is no mutual trust between the statutory and voluntary sector.

This inevitably affects the way voluntary services relate to clients and the service they are able to provide. This needs to be changed.

Voluntary organisations need recognition, more support and to be heard. Statutory bodies need to be more innovative and imaginative, and genuine in their relationships. Improvements in relationships should be focused on trust and respect.

Voluntary organisations have a responsibility to recognise the limitations they face and to say no, enough is enough. This is the work that we want to do, but these are the resources and support we need in order to achieve it.

Voluntary services need to draw up an agenda for services for black people. How do we tell the purse holder what we want? How do we create a positive relationship with statutory organisations?"

The opening remarks set the scene in enabling all the participants to discuss, in their workshops, the question of building links and working together with health and local authorities as well as the voluntary sector.

Workshop leaders' directives were to try and 'focus-down' with experiences from people's own areas of how links could be developed and maintained and what were some of the hurdles that would need to be negotiated.

This, therefore, is the final summary of feedback from all the participants.

VOLUNTARY AND STATUTORY SERVICES WORKING TOGETHER

Facilitators for the six workshops were: Mike Silvera, Yvonne Christie, Juliana Frederick, Peter Ferns, Loraine Martins and Adrian Williams.

The issue of white projects and organisations setting up black initiatives and employing black people to gain organisational credibility and resources was raised. When organisations are forced by financial constraints to make cutbacks, these projects and the black workers are often the first to go. The situation in MIND South East was quoted as just one example. Their Black and Minority Unit did not gain continued funding and in fact was closed down. White projects have always been in a more advantageous position than black projects to attract funding. With reduced resources this situation is worsening.

Most black organisations were developed out of a lack of appropriate services and so adopt a campaigning approach. They now face the dilemma of what to do with their campaigning and advocacy functions. These organisations have in the past relied on local authority funding but will not now be able to do so under terms laid out by the new contracting system.

General practitioner services are not aware of and do not make good use of the local voluntary organisations such as psychotherapy counselling. Their use would inevitably result in less call out time and less wasted finances.

The medical model of treating the symptoms and not the whole person is unsatisfactory. Clients are expected to resume life in the community with no skills or opportunities to lead a normal life.

The fourteen Regional Health Authorities should be encouraged to have Black Health Forums. Membership should be as wide as possible and their primary function would be to feed a black perspective into services, and to develop training and new initiatives. Their guidelines and criteria should be developed by local black people. The forum should be really race reflective, and not just reflect the largest black communities in their area.

WHERE DO WE GO FROM HERE?

Throughout the conference there were seven consistent themes, all of which were inter-related.

CONSULTATION

Most agencies in health and social welfare provide a uniform service to the whole population. Where individuals and communities have differing needs, this approach results in unequal service for some sections of the population.

The voice of the user has been increasing in recent years. Black people have been putting their case forward for more appropriate services for a long time, but are yet to have much influence on the services. There is little evidence that positive steps are being taken to bridge the gulf in communication between services and the black communities and to incorporate their views into the planning process.

The voluntary sector has been grossly under-represented on Joint Care Planning Teams and these have recently been even further reduced. Black representation on them is virtually non-existent.

The whole voluntary sector needs to become more involved in consultation and planning structures. The black community, including those of its members who work within statutory organisations, cannot afford to wait for its needs to be recognised. We need to organise an effective lobby. A strategy to initiate the maximum amount of pressure and influence on decision makers is called for.

PUBLIC EDUCATION

There is a need to raise issues concerning the implications of the Community Care Act for the black community. Campaigning methods such as extensive use of the local media (radio and television) and leafletting are advocated. Targeting particular areas would yield better results, as would contacting people where they usually meet, such as in schools and community centres. Lobbying Members of Parliament is also important. Mention was made of the Community Care Alliance of Black Voluntary Organisations. They have an information and campaigning function around the Community Care Act. They will be in existence only until April 1991. There is a need to find more practical measures to keep this issue on the agenda.

Attitudes to mental health in the black communities are neither informed nor positive. The media should be utilised to the maximum, and local radio programmes targeted at black communities should have discussions on mental health. Emphasis should be placed on mental health rather than mental illness; our rights within the mental health regulations; the need to challenge the way services currently operate against black people; and the value and limitation of alternative therapies.

SUPPORT FOR BLACK WORKERS

Black workers are potentially the key people in the provision of more accessible and appropriate services to black communities. The dilemma facing them is a constant area of concern.

It should not be assumed that all black staff are committed and skilled in working in an anti-racist way. They will have had the same training and are subjected to the same professional norms and role models as their white colleagues and will not necessarily be skilled, confident and supported sufficiently to develop this way of working. Many others have become known as the 'race experts' which relieves white staff of their moral and professional responsibilities. Their approaches and perspectives are not always recognised. Those employed specifically as specialist race advisors often have unclear job descriptions and are working to a very large remit. The racism in the system is overwhelming and these workers are 'set up to fail'.

Black workers' support groups within white organisations would give black workers confidence, and enable them to have a voice, and to support each other. This is viewed as a code of good practice in employment, but some authorities are not facilitating the development of such groups. The health service has a poor track record in this area.

Black workers should aim for solidarity with local communities. This will not only provide support, but may help protect them from hostilities within the organisation. Such groups should aim to identify allies and identify where their political, social and financial supports lie.

NETWORKING

Black workers in both voluntary and statutory services should develop networks with each other through contacts, liaison and communication on an individual basis.

Those who have specialist posts within these organisations can use their positions to maximum advantage if they link up with community networks. Networks should include meeting on issues such as mental health.

The challenge is how can we make networking more effective and more relevant to our work experiences.

COLLECTIVE ACTION

Collective action could strengthen our representation to statutory organisations and make it more effective. The challenge is how to do this under the pressure of such rapid and multiple changes and have meagre resources.

There is a call for a consortia, such as the National Black Mental Health Association, to include black workers in the statutory and voluntary sectors as well as users and carers. Statutory resources could be used to service this forum.

Statutory sector workers could be involved in supporting voluntary organisations. This has to be done with caution and in an innovative manner to maintain confidentiality and avoid breach of contract.

The different organisations involved would not necessarily have to agree on everything. It is the dialogue that is important. Such an organisation would have a role in reducing the competition between black organisations for scarce resources and would guard against organisations being exploited by funders in their attempts at spending.

INFORMATION EXCHANGE

There is no shortage of models and ideas for addressing black people's care needs. What is lacking is the mechanism and structure to promote the sharing of information.

An information exchange would ensure that people were kept up to date on issues affecting their communities and on the numerous events and initiatives being undertaken in all sectors. The Fanon Project in Brixton is willing to be involved in this. The National Community Health Resource has a black worker to co-ordinate black community health initiatives. It also has a Black Health Forum which provides information and support for black workers involved in community health initiatives.

It is recognised that initiatives and resources are based mainly in London and workers may find it difficult to participate and gain access. A more proactive stance should be taken and developed through outreach work. Organisations such as the King's Fund Centre and MIND could help to resource this.

To facilitate an information exchange, a list of all the conference delegates is given in Appendix B.

TRAINING

If anti-racist policies are to be effective, training will be needed at all levels. Some reference was made to the training of the police to enable them to work in a more anti-racist way. However, the type of training which was consistently called for was for black staff.

Black service providers may lack awareness and understanding of what racism is, and how it affects both their position in the organisation and the service they provide to black clients. At present, there is little access to training which enables black staff to improve their personal effectiveness under such circumstances and to see themselves as potential advocates for black service users.

Such training does not always necessarily mean bringing in outside trainers. A considerable amount of skill and knowledge can be gained from other black workers within the system.

The black voluntary sector needs to understand how the system works and to use local authorities more creatively. Training within voluntary organisations should be given a higher priority, and focus should include the following areas:

- ✦ mental health rather than mental illness
- ✦ preparation of grant applications
- ✦ networking skills
- ✦ management training:
  - running organisations
  - budgets
  - accountability
  - manager/worker relationships.

THE ROLE OF THE KING'S FUND CENTRE

The King's Fund Centre is well known as an information resource. It aims to develop and maintain links with projects in the statutory sector as well as with local and national voluntary organisations. A national information exchange is being developed at the Centre, funded by the Department of Health. The Community Living Development Team are keen to fill gaps in services and would be willing to organise conferences, seminars and training on the issue of mental health. Free places on these would be offered to users and carers.

NATIONAL GROUP

The newly-formed National Black Mental Health Group is one forum taking the issues forward. They will be holding their meetings in different parts of the country to service as many new black mental health initiatives as possible.

LESSONS OF THE CONFERENCE

INVOLVEMENT AND PARTNERSHIPS WITH USERS

There were some disappointments from which we will continue to learn and grow.

The main disappointment was our failure to make this conference truly useful for service users. When organising events, it is important to try to involve a range of people from the beginning. It is also crucial to try to be aware of differences in experiences and expectations. It is wrong to assume that the presence of several service users means that is enough in itself, given the unequal power relationships between providers and users. Some service providers constantly referred to themselves as professionals, which itself immediately draws dividing lines between them and their clients. Positive steps should be taken to empower service users so that they are able actively to contribute, participate and learn. Service providers were asked to bring users who must have summoned up a considerable amount of courage and trust to attend. However, several users did not return on the second day. Contribution from users suggested that sometimes the language which was adopted excluded them. For example, both service providers and users would have found the research findings which were presented interesting, but the highly technical nature of the data precluded that. It was suggested that this information be made available at a later date in a simpler form.

STRUCTURE AND ORGANISATION OF THE CONFERENCE

Another issue of concern was the lack of success, despite the measures taken, to make this an all black conference. The ethnic monitoring questions used were not able to ensure that all delegates (either as voluntary and statutory service providers, as well as users) were from black communities. Black communities are still relatively inexperienced at requesting and securing space for themselves. While recognising that this is a privilege which will remain largely dependent on the goodwill of white people, there is a need to continue to explore more creative and effective ways of achieving this.

Finally, maintaining the right balance between a highly structured didactic and formal workshop in which participants 'do as they are told', and the more participative approach of involving them in determining the course of events, can often be difficult. Participants will also have different needs and expectations about this. Concerns about lack of structure (from a minority of participants) may well be a reflection of these differing needs. Would the former approach have yielded the degree of intense feeling and emotion needed to improve commitment to urgent action? Did the need for a more information based conference leave some participants without the data and confidence they require to develop these issues further with their managers within white organisations?

The 'right balance' will come closer to being realised by using a variety of methods, and more flexibility and choice for participants.

A FINAL WORD

A most valuable aspect of the two days was the opportunity to share experiences and ideas in a "safe" environment. This is vividly depicted in the feedback from one workshop:

> *Free to be me*
> *Despite the broken dreams*
> *Sharing my frustrations*
> *Accepted by you all.*
>
> *We may not agree*
> *Our paths may never cross*
> *But in the midst of all the gloom*
> *You allowed me to be me.*

We cannot afford to see ourselves merely as victims and as passive recipients of mediocre reforms. We have never been ones for sitting back and allowing our rights and dignity to be violated, and that same magnitude of resistance is called for in the field of mental health.

Many conference participants left after the two days charged for action. Action is, however, needed from all sides and on all fronts. To those readers of this report who did not have the opportunity to be involved in this workshop, we hope that the report will be of help to you in taking the issues forward.

SUMMARY OF RECOMMENDATIONS

This summary of the main recommendations is not meant to be read alone, but in conjunction with the main body of the report. However, to assist those charged with the future development of the service, a listing of recommendations may be of some use.

PERSPECTIVES OF THE NHS AND COMMUNITY CARE ACT

1. Black service providers have a responsibility to feed into care plans. They should not be viewed, however, as acting on behalf of black communities.

2. A consortia of black organisations is recommended. This will not only strengthen but also guard against organisations having to compete against each other for scarce resources.

SUPPORTING AND INVOLVING FAMILIES IN THE COMMUNITY

1. Carers should be involved in care plans from the beginning and should be encouraged to keep involved. This is particularly important in view of the shift towards community care.

2. There is a need to encourage the setting up of carers groups. This will facilitate black carers to organise effective advocacy groups and networks.

3. More community projects should be established for users to provide some respite for carers.

4. The black community should make links with the local media to make the issues facing them known.

5. There is an urgent need for more information from health authorities about drugs, their side effects and how to avoid dependency on prescribed medication.

6.   Joint funding to facilitate a 24-hour crisis service is needed.

7.   A clearer policy on using Section 136 of the Mental Health Act is needed.

8.   More appropriate definitions of 'place of safety' are required.

9.   The police should receive training in anti-racist ways of working, with particular reference to their role in mental health services.

ALTERNATIVE THERAPIES

1.   There is an urgent need for information about alternative therapies within black communities. Emphasis should be on outlining both the scope of this form of therapy, its appropriate uses, and its limitations.

2.   Evaluation and monitoring should be measured in case studies alongside those of mainstream medical practice.

3.   Black communities should not lose confidence in their own traditional therapeutic approaches such as spiritual treatment and counselling.

BLACK WOMEN AND MENTAL HEALTH

The diagram on page 15 was presented by workshop participants as a summary of the issues they discussed and where action needs to take place in working towards better mental health for black women.

MENTAL HEALTH AND THE ELDERLY

1.   There is a need for more research into the extent and nature of mental illness among black elders.

2.   Good interpreter and advocacy services should be developed to help improve access to and quality of services.

VOLUNTARY AND STATUTORY SERVICES WORKING TOGETHER

1. Voluntary organisations should become involved in available quality auditing as detailed under the Community Care Act.

2. General Practitioners should be encouraged to develop links with and make better use of black voluntary organisations.

3. Services should prepare clients with mental health problems for employment and community living.

4. A crisis service needs to be developed to provide cover at evenings and weekends. This should be well resourced with crisis intervention workers, including personnel with an in-depth understanding of mental health, as well as the wider issues concerning racism and social factors.

    There should be some degree of flexibility, providing various options to meet the needs of the particular individual.

5. Active steps should be taken to recruit more black front line workers.

6. Voluntary sectors must work with all statutory sectors. This includes local authority, health authority, the police, prison and probation services.

APPENDIX A

ORGANISATIONS AND PROJECTS REFERRED TO IN THIS REPORT

Afro-Caribbean Mental Health Association
35-37 Electric Avenue
Brixton
LONDON
SW9 8JP
Tel 071-737 3603/4

Community Care Alliance of Black Voluntary Organisations
c/o LVSC
68 Charlton Street
LONDON
NW1 1JR
Tel 081-388 0241

Contact: Adrian Williams

Fanon Project
33 Effra Road
Brixton
LONDON SW2
Tel 071-274 2513 or 071-737 2888

Focus Consultancy
Bon Marche Buildings
444 Brixton Road
LONDON SW9 8EH
SW1X 7PQ
Tel 071-737 7155

Contact: Josephine Kwahli

Hackney Afro-Caribbean Mental Health Programme
Hackney Social Services Department
205 Morning Lane
LONDON
E9 6JX
Tel 081-986 3123 ext 4777

Contact: George Escoffrey

King's Fund Centre
126 Albert Street
LONDON
NW1 7NF
Tel 071-267 6111

Contact: Yvonne Christie

Mental Health Shop
67 Regent Road
LEICESTER
Tel 0533-471525

MIND
22 Harley Street
LONDON
W1N 2ED
Tel 071-637 0741

National Community Health Resource
57 Charlton Street
LONDON
NW1 1HU
Tel 071-383 3841

Contact: Mercy Jeyasingham

APPENDIX B

CONFERENCE ORGANISATION

Yvonne Christie
Senior Project Officer
King's Fund Centre
126 Albert Street
LONDON NW1 7NF   Tel 071-267 6111

Peter Ferns
London Boroughs Training Committee
9 Tavistock Place
LONDON WC1H 9SN   Tel 071-388 2041

Juliana Frederick
Black Mental Health Group
The Playtower
Ladywell Road
LONDON   SE13 7UW   Tel 081-314 1660

Loraine Martins
Afro-Caribbean Unit
LVSC
68 Chalton Street
LONDON   NW1 1JR   Tel 071-388 0241

Arunjot Mushiana
National Schizophrenia Fellowship
197 King's Cross Road
LONDON   WC1X 9BZ   Tel 071-837 6436

Mike Silvera
Parkside Health Authority
District Headquarters
16 South Wharf Road
LONDON W2 1PF   Tel 071-725 1959

Adrian Williams
Afro-Caribbean Unit
LVSC
68 Chalton Street
LONDON   NW1 1JR   Tel 071-388 0241

APPENDIX C

CONFERENCE PROGRAMME

The Future of Mental Health Services for the Black Communities

Day One – Wednesday, 19 September 1990

10.00am   Registration and Coffee (in Foyer)

10.30am   Welcome – Aims of the Conference
                 Yvonne Christie, King's Fund Centre

10.40am   Guest Speakers:

            i) Josephine Kwahli
                – Focus Consultancy

            ii) Dr Aggrey Burke
                – St George's Hospital

Questions and input from all participants

12.00pm   LUNCH

1.30   Workshops:

            a) Women and Mental Health

            b) Mental Health and the Elderly

            c) Perspectives on the White Paper

            d) Alternative Therapies

            e) Mental Health Services in the Community

            f) Caring and Involving Families

3.00pm   Feedback from Workshops (5 minutes each)

3.30pm	TEA
4.00pm	Workshops
5.30 - 6.00pm	Feedback from Workshops
6.30 - 7.30pm	DINNER
8.00pm	Informal get together

Day Two – Thursday, 20 September 1990

9.45am	Coffee
10.15am	Overview of first day Yvonne Christie, King's Fund Centre
10.30am*	Guest Speaker Stephanie Gabriel, Bristol Inner City Mental Health Project

Questions and input from all participants

11.00am	Coffee (in foyer)
11.30am	Workshops – all to discuss voluntary and statutory sectors working together to effect charges (6 groups)
1.30pm	Exchange and feedback as a large group
2.00	LUNCH
3.00	Where do we go from here? – 1 large group Mike Silvera
4.00	Summing up the conference Yvonne Christie
4.15	End – Safe Journey

* *Unfortunately at the last moment, Stephanie Gabriel was not able to attend. The session was led instead by Loraine Martins – Director, ACCDU.*

Guest Speakers

Dr Aggrey Burke
Senior Lecturer
St George's Hospital Medical School
Department of Psychiatry
Jenner Wing
Cranmer Terrace
Tooting
LONDON   SW17 ORE   Tel 081-672 9944

Josephine Kwahli
Director of Social Division
Bon Marche Buildings
444 Brixton Road
LONDON   SW9 8EJ   Tel 071-737 7155

Facilitators

Dr Pearl Hetteriarchy
Consultant Psychiatrist
Winchester Health Authority
St Paul's Hospital
WINCHESTER
Hants   SO22 5AA   Tel 0962-60661
                                     x 2003

Mark I
Community Liaison Worker
17 Clifton Mansions
429 Coldharbour Lane
Brixton
LONDON   SW9 8LL   Tel 081-854 8888
                                     x 3102

Loraine Martins
Director
Afro-Caribbean Community Development Unit
LVSC
68 Chalton Street
LONDON   NW1 1JR   Tel 071-388 0241

Safder Mohammed
Development Worker
Primary Health Care Group
King's Fund Centre
126 Albert Street
London NW1 7NF   Tel 071-267 6111

Dr. Parimala Moodley
Director
Maudsley Hospital Outreach Support Team (MOST)
5 Camberwell Church Street
Camberwell
LONDON   SE5   Tel 071-708 2040

Ms Arunjot Mushiana
Development Officer
National Schizophrenia Fellowship
197 King's Cross Road
LONDON   WC1X 9BZ   Tel 071-837 6436

Ms Angela Powell
Co-ordinator
Handsworth Community Centre
The Villa Methodist Church
Villa Road and Rose Hill
Handsworth
BIRMINGHAM   B21 9AR   Tel 021-554 4755

Kiron Sandhu
Co-ordinator
Forward Project
c/o Project Enterprise
16 Askew Crescent
Shepherd's Bush
LONDON   W12   Tel 081-740 7271

Mike Silvera
Purchasing Manager
Parkside Health Authority
16 South Wharf Road
W2 1PK   Tel 071-725 1959

Adrian Williams
Development Officer
Afro-Caribbean Community Development Unit
LVSC
68 Chalton Street
LONDON   NW1 1JR   Tel 071-388 0241

Lydia Yee
Development Officer
Carers Unit
King's Fund Centre
126 Albert Street
LONDON NW1 7NF   Tel 071-267 6111

Mike Zamora
Development Officer
Social Services Area 2
820 Seven Sisters Road
Tottenham
LONDON   N15   Tel 081-809 4466

APPENDIX D

LIST OF PARTICIPANTS

AWADZI Prospero	Unity Helpline
AMBROSE Anthea	Leicestershire County Council
BAPTISTE June	Women in Greenwich
BARRETT Margaret	ACEP Womens Centre
BARTELS-ELLIS Phillida	White City Mental Health Project
BELL Fabiola	London Borough of Haringey
BENJAMIN Lloyd	Participant
BHABUTA Anju	Liverpool Health Promotion Unit
BOLTON Margaret	London Boroughs Grants Unit
BOYE Margo	Pupil Barrister
BROOKS Anna	Moss Side Health Centre
BROOKS Cynthia	MOST
CADDICK Pauline	Merseyside Community Relations Council
CHANDLER Sharon	Greenwich MIND Networks
CHUDASANA Karson	East Birmingham Mental Health
CLARK Dunstan	Moss Side Social Services Dept
CUMMINGS James	Croydon Race and Community Unit
DANJI Mary	Brent MIND
DEMETRIOU Pani	Haringey Social Services
EDWARDS Geraldine	Ravenswood Housing Trust

EGOH Ejaeta	Southwark Phoenix Womens Health
EGOH Joyce	Southwark Phoenix Womens Health
ESCOFFERY George	Hackney Social Services
EYERS Rose	Greenwich MIND Networks
FERGUSON Gilroy	ACMHG Project
FOSTER Amber	London Borough of Haringey SSD
FREDERICK Luciana	London Borough of Haringey SSD
GODDARD Kathy	Brent Social Services Department
GRAHAM Joan	Womens Equality Unit
GRANDISON Vere	Croydon Race and Community Unit
HALL Peter	The Fanon Project
HANNEY David	HAS
HARRISON Chris	Good Practices in Mental Health
HAYNES Ricardo	Ravenswood Housing Trust
HUSSAIN Shahida	London Borough of Waltham Forest
IFINNWA Esther	Greenwich MIND Networks
JACK Cameron	UJIMA Housing Association
JEYASINGHAM Mercy	NCHR
JOSEPH Sonia	Hackney Black Peoples Association
JOHN-BAPTISTE Grace	Greenwich MIND Social Services
JOHNS Trevor	Greenwich MIND Networks
KABANDA Rebecca	African/Caribbean Mental Health Organisation
KOAY Shirley	Bloomsbury Health Authority
KOUNOUDIS Chris	Parkside CHC

MAHABEER Raj	Ealing Hospital, St. Bernards
MANNING Linda	Oxfordshire Health Unit
MATTHEW Paul	Leicester Black Mental Health Group
MAYNARD Yvonne	London Borough of Brent
McNISH Donald	MOST
MIRZANIA Bassi	Ealing Health Authority
MITCHELL Elaine	Voluntary
MITCHELL-BARNES Jane	Black and Ethnic Communities Mental Health Project
MORGAN Vivienne	Westminster MIND
NANDA Geeta	Man Sangathan
NEVINS Peter	Islington MIND
NIND Pamela	MIND in Ealing
OSHOKO Olu	Participant
PARKER Ann	Bloomsbury Community Health Council
RAMSEY-McINTOSH Maxine	Lewisham Social Services Dept
SANDHU Jayne	Leicester Action for Mental Health
SEALY Jacqui	Mental Health Shop
SHAMASH Michael	London Borough of Camden SSD
SMALL Frank	London Borough of Islington
SUNU Kofi	London Borough of Hammersmith and Fulham SSD
WADIA Avan	Shanti Womens Counselling Service

APPENDIX E

FURTHER READING

1. A Report of a Seminar on Community Care for the Mental Health of Black and Ethnic Minority Senior Citizens. Standing Conference of Ethnic Minority Senior Citizens, 1985.

2. Baker R (ed) (1983): Psychosocial Problems of Refugees. The British Refugee Council and European Consultation on Refugees and Exiles.

3. Blakemore K (1983): Health and illness among the elderly of minority ethnic groups living in Birmingham: some new findings. Health Trends, pp 69-72, August.

4. Brandon D (1981): Mental health and ethnic minorities. North West MIND.

5. Burke A (ed) (1989): Racism and Mental Illness. Transcultural Psychiatry Society.

6. Burke A (ed) (1984): Racism and Mental Illness. International Journal of Social Psychiatry, Spring.

7. Burke A (1986): Racism, Prejudice and Mental Illness. In Cox J (ed) Transcultural Psychiatry, pp 139-157, Croom Helm, London.

8. Carpenter L & Brockington I F (1980): A study of mental illness in Asians, West Indians and Africans living in Manchester. British Journal of Psychiatry, vol 137, pp 201-205.

9. Chesler P (1972): Women and Madness. Avon, New York.

10. Christie Y (1990): Race and Mental Health. In King's Fund Newsletter, Vol 13, No. 3, September.

11. Christie Y, Blunden R (1991): Is Race on your Agenda? King's Fund Centre.

12. Commission for Racial Equality (1976): Mental Health among minority ethnic groups. CRE.

13. Community Relations Commission (1976): Aspects of Mental Health in a Multicultural Society.

14. Cox J (1986): Transcultural Psychiatry. Croom Helm, London.

15. Directory of Black and Ethnic Community Mental Health Services in London: Voluntary Sector. Produced by Laurence Ward, MIND South East.

16. Fanon F (1986): Black Skin, White Masks. Pluto Press, London.

17. Fernando S (1986): Depression in Ethnic Minorities. In Cox J (ed) Transcultural Psychiatry, pp 107-138. Croom Helm, London.

18. Giggs J (1973): High rates of schizophrenia among immigrants in Nottingham. Nursing Times, 20 September, pp 1210-1212.

19. Goldberg D, Huxley P: Mental Illness in the Community. The pathway to psychiatric care. Tavistock Publications, London.

20. Gostin L (1986): Institutions Observed: Towards a new concept of provision in mental health. King's Fund, London.

21. Harrison G et al (1988): A prospective study of severe mental disorder in African-Caribbean patients. Psychological Medicine 18, pp 643-657.

22. Hitch P (1981): Immigrants and mental health: local research and social explorations. New Community, 9, No.2, pp 256-262.

23. Lago C (1981): Cross-cultural counselling: some developments, thoughts and hypotheses. New Community, 9, no.1, pp 59-63.

24. Littlewood and Lipsedge M (1982): Alients and Alienists: ethnic minorities and psychiatry.

25. Mental Health among Minority Ethnic Groups. Commission for Racial Equality.

26. Murphy H B M (1977): Migration, culture and mental health. Psychological Medicine, 7, pp 677-684.

27. Penfold P S & Walker G A (1984): Women and the Psychiatric Paradox. Open University Press.

28. Protect their minds too: stress among ethnic minority groups. Mind Out, November/December 1978, pp 12-14.

29. Racism is a number one mental health problem: racial minorities and the Mental Health Act. Mind Out, May 1981, pp 3-5.

30. Rack, P A (1978): Stress among immigrants. Stress Today, December.

31. Rack P (1982): Race, Culture and Mental Disorder. Tavistock Publications.

32. Ramon S (ed) (1988): Psychiatry in Transition: The British and Italian Experiences. Pluto Press, London.

33. Sills A, Taylor G & Golding P (1988): The Politics of the Urban Crisis. Hutchinson, London.

34. Snowden L R (ed): Reaching the Underserved: Mental Health Needs of Neglected populations. Sage Publications.

35. Steadman H J (1983): Predicting dangerousness among the mentally ill: art, magic, science. International Journal of Law and Psychiatry 6, pp 381-390.

36. Thomas A & Sillen S (1979): Racism and Psychiatry. Citadel Press, New Jersey.

37. Westwood S et al (1989): Sadness in My Heart: Racism and Mental Health – A Research Report. Leicester Black Mental Health Group, University of Leicester.

38. Willie C V, Kramer B M & Brown B S (eds) (1973): Racism and Mental Health. University of Pittsburgh Press.